SISTE VIATOR

ALSO BY SARAH MANGUSO

The Captain Lands in Paradise

Free Radicals: American Poets Before Their First Books
(coedited with Jordan Davis)

SISTE VIATOR

poems by

SARAH MANGUSO

Four Way Books
New York City

Distributed by
University Press of New England
Hanover and London

Editorial Office
Four Way Books
POB 535, Village Station
New York, NY 10014
www.fourwaybooks.com

Library of Congress Catalogue Card Number: 2004113816
ISBN: 1-884800-69-6

Cover art: Heidi Neilson, *Cloud Cube,* 2000.
Photo collage, 18 x 22 inches. Courtesy of the artist.

Book cover design: Cubanica.

Photo of Sarah Manguso © Marion Ettlinger.

This book is manufactured in the United States of America and printed on acid-free paper.

Four Way Books is a not-for-profit organization. We are grateful for the assistance we receive from individual donors, foundations, and government arts agencies.

This publication is made possible with public funds from the New York State Council on the Arts, a state agency.

Distributed by University Press of New England
One Court Street, Lebanon, NH 03766

We are a proud member of the Council of Literary Magazines and Presses.

ACKNOWLEDGMENTS

Grateful acknowledgment is made to the editors of the journals
and anthologies in which some of these poems first appeared,
sometimes in slightly different forms:

*The American Poetry Review, Barrow Street, Blackbird, Blue
Mesa Review, Boston Review, can we have our ball back?, The
Columbia Poetry Review, Conduit, Denver Quarterly, Ecotone,
Explosive, Forklift, KultureFlash, Kulture Vulture, The London
Review of Books, McSweeney's Internet Tendency, New American
Writing, New England Review, The New Review of Literature,
Now Culture, The Paris Review, Pleiades, Ploughshares, Poets.org,
Spout, Tin House, Volt, Washington Square, Western Humanities
Review.*

"Address from One Place to Another," "An Idea with No Bodily
Counterpart," "The Dictionary," "The Haunted Igloo" "Hell,"
"Love Letter (Clouds)," "The Ten Thousand," "They Are
Unlike Us in Almost Every Other Way," "The Trick Is Not
Minding," and "What Concerns Me Now" appeared in the
anthology *Poetry 30* (Ed. Gerry LaFemina, Mammoth Books,
2005).

"Hell" appeared in *Best American Poetry of 2005* (Ed. Paul Muldoon,
series ed. David Lehman, Scribner, 2005).

"Nepenthe" appeared in *Great American Prose Poems: From Poe to
the Present* (Ed. David Lehman, Scribner, 2003).

The author would like to thank The Council of the Humanities
at Princeton University, The Jentel Artist Residency Program,
Sally Ball and Martha Rhodes at Four Way Books, Domenick
Ammirati, Catherine Barnett, Catherine Corman, Jordan
Davis, Joy Katz, Jennifer L. Knox, and Michael Savitz for their
generous help.

Siste viator (Stop, traveler)
was a common inscription
on Roman roadside tombs.

TABLE OF CONTENTS

EVERYTHING

Before I gave my eyes to a liar with ruined entrails
I saw the shape for the fifteenth time.

I thought I saw how the story got told.
And I gave it everything.

Blind I listen to all the little sounds.
How pretty they are.
I arrive and arrive.
Look—I am the statue that thinks it's running.

ASKING FOR MORE

I am not asking to suffer less.
I hope to be nearly crucified.
To live because I don't want to.

That hope, that sweet agent—
My best work is *its* work.
The horse I ride into Hell is my best horse
And bears its name.
So, friends, drink your cocktails and wear your hats.
Thank you for leaving me this whole world to go mad in.

I am not asking for mercy. I am asking for *more*.
I don't mind when no mercy comes
Or when it comes in the form of my mad self
Running at me. I am not asking for mercy.

THIS MIGHT BE REAL

How long in a cold room will the tea stay hot?
What about reality interests you?
How long can you live?
Were you there when I said *this might be real*?
How much do you love?
Sixty percent?
Things that are gone?
Do you love what's real?
Is real a partial form?
Is it a nascent form?
What is it before it's real?
Is it a switch that moves and then is ever still?
Is it a spectrum of cross-fades?
Is what's next *real*?
When it comes will everything turn real?
If I drink enough tea to hallucinate, is that real?
If I know I'm waiting for someone but I don't know who, is he real?
Is he real when he comes?
Is he real when he's gone?
Is consequence what's real?
Is consequence all that's real?
What brings consequence?
Is *it* what's real?
Is *it* what turned everything to disbelief, the last form love takes?

CIVIC PRIDE

I cleared my throat and found I had swallowed my civic pride.
My gorge smarting, I stood up in the town
And put on some scaffolding and Tyvek
That floated around me like a curtain
Into which a breeze whispers a dirty joke.
I found a citizen in the town,
God he loves this city. He loves it so much
He lies down on me to put out the fire
When he finds me standing in flame.
Despite him the fire spreads to surrounding lots.
The golden figure at the top of the municipal building—
The angel on my hat that signals Civic Pride
To all who lift their gaze heavenward—
Comforts me in my inferno. The fire is beautiful.
I don't know who lit this fire.

GETTING OVER THE TWENTIETH CENTURY

At first it just sat on its pages, crying at me.

The twentieth century let me discover it.

I loved it so much I tattooed a hundred-year calendar on my wrist.

Its space exploration and its acid trips are what I miss most,

and I want to go back even though the possibility of time travel
   was already gone by its third decade.

At times I pity it, a century lost inside another one like a toy boat
   floating in the pump room.

Almost no one goes in there.

Though the twentieth century is unlikely to be found again as I
   found it a hundred years ago, it will be,

and when that happens I will become lost as the boat's wake that
   is, for a moment, indeed real

but is replaced then by another wake, similar but not the same—
   not ever the same.

And I will disappear, by then made almost entirely of history,
   the way history itself disappears leaving only its memory to
   be ruined by the captains of a new, distracted age.

Jupiter Has Sixty-One Moons

There's no difference between writing down what you hear and writing down what you wish you heard.

On Jupiter there are sixty-one colors, one for each moon. Painting students make moon-studies in their first color lessons.

It's hard to see in the dark, as it is for hours each day. Painters are taught to paint blindfolded. Talented colorists show themselves during this exercise.

When they do, they are taken away, as they suffer from a disease that only light can cure.

Reverence

Love not the rider but the old rider,
The ghost in the saddle: Obey that ghost.
A good horse runs even at the shadow of the whip.
But we are not good horses.
We bolt. We stand still in bad weather.
We rely on things we know are unreliable,
It feels so good just to *rely*.
We are relied on.
But I don't know who knows that bad secret.
I don't see who sits astride my back,
Who cuts my flank so lovingly on our way to the dark mountain.

Justice for the Undelivered

I'm set free
I'm here to set you free

From the bright horror
Of the last thing you enjoyed

Please stay
Until the next experience

Where there is justice
There's not always the idea of justice

In sociology as well as in biology
Evolution may be accidental

Thanks to time
Mastery of a form means something new each moment

Unless the idea of that form is fixed
And then mastery is possible

But industry toward attainable goals
Is self-limiting

Yet sloth kills
As quickly as overwork

Surrender
Is how at least one major religion translates

And how much you yield to anything
Determines how much you enjoy it

Please stay
Take a little walk with me and let us get truly lost

EST, EST, EST

The discovery of Italy's best wine,
and not alcohol poisoning, is what killed the prelate.

You've got to hide your love away,
not because showing it is useless,

but because it isn't.
Don't let me get what I want.

I love you as dead people love—in every way imaginable.
Don't let me bring that cat inside.

If you leave your wife with her beautiful name,
don't tell me.

See this deer track?
Just walk away.

When he had any, Dostoyevsky threw away his money.
I won't let you in my house.

THE BLACK GARDEN

The first thing I did was imagine a circle and get in it.
Outside the circle the world waited
With its dinner party and its hologram floor of moving stars.

●

Why is it called thus
The tourists asked the inhabitant.
Nothing grew or died there,
And they could not see where the circle ended and began.
I am the only one who can see it.
I am a lonely albino, I pour dark tea down my gullet
All day long just so they can see me.

●

Today I woke up, juggled, made a few notes,
And became symbolically suicidal.
My juggling-balls are shaped like stars.

●

Where are you if not outside the enclosure?
Only figments live inside.
I am colorless and cold, I am my own figment.

PRAYER

Her lover returns, and she hails their love as finally unassailable,
   as *life in death*.

This is the place religion occupies in her life. Its reach goes no further.

I have prayed the orange ladybug that has lain between the window
   sashes all winter is only sleeping.

God, you have never forsaken me.

Prayer—for a long time music was the closest thing to it.

Sometimes one need only seat oneself a few feet deeper into a room.

The blue of my typewriter is profound, its density foreign even
   to the sky.

Writing is work with such a machine. Is prayer.

Music was the closest thing to it.

I try to explain to a friend who lives by reason that she does not
   live by faith and is therefore not a believer.

Pretending to mean something.
Pretending to believe something.
Pretending to believe in something.

These people profess to love a song but cannot even approximate
   the tune.

They must not love the songs they say they love.

Yet what they remember *is* what the girl sings on the bright stage.

14

What Concerns Me Now

What concerns me now is already done.
Predictions are wasted on me.

What concerns me now is waking up ecstatically
As when the cat meows the whole day and then grows quiet
Or the king takes off his crown and rolls it down the hill.

Physicists write of two possible fates of the universe,
Each dependent on a hypothetical amount of dark matter.
The two amounts are described as *a small amount* and *a large amount.*

The more complicated things become,
The simpler they are to understand
When explained by someone who already understands them.

What isn't like this?

What concerns me now is this drag queen shouting her monologue
    into the sky
Which is not so much *there* as it is visible to the tourists that walk
    under it.

Who can say when *act* becomes *light?*

The sun, a rictus in that sky—
Encoded with the outer limit of life on Earth, the ultimate death's
    head.

What concerns me now is this need to stop lying.
The so-called pain that fills my heart is actually located elsewhere.
As for the heart, it's nothing but empty space
And all it ever fills with is my own blood.

What concerns me now is this large animal swimming lovingly
    toward me.

A FLAG-RAISING

Those with identities got the whole cake of soap
And, after that, the whole cake.
The title shortened itself when I wasn't looking.

I spend a good part of the day sitting on a black raft.
Above me floats a burning clock. A blue flag.
I'm good only for waiting and, after that, only for arriving.

I'm trying to climb out of an analgesic bath.
Attendants keep adding to it.
I need to describe this bath.
It is like a raft in itself. It is like a summoning.

I spend a good part of the day.
Stop, traveler! It's time to reheat the bath.
Call over to that bevy of sailors.
Let them raise the flag.

ICE-LYRIC

I left town to escape the burning triumvirate
But it followed me in the form of a dirty sheet
With my name on it three times in cross-stitch
Which smothered doubt.

The only direction I remembered was north.
The usual junk had stopped working
And I anticipated a replacement junk
Somewhere in their 777 words for snow.

Reader, where does inclusion stop?
Where in the snow is the junk of the answer?

—When it realizes it is exclusion.

—It is in the snowman's sooty entrails, and in his sooty heart.

THERE IS SUCH A THING

I spoke to fire as to a bright lover in the forest
Whose brightness was for me.
And fire made everything into itself—
The forest, the cabin, the bed, the book—
And it bore me, a horse of fire bore me
Across the hot river.
It burned my lungs but did not change me.
It was gone and I cried for it as for my best horse,
My love and what would not change me.

The Ten Thousand

The ten thousand stand before us.
My back is marked with my blood but I can't see it.
In this way a greater perspective is alluded to.
The ten thousand cannot see the blood on the back of my neck.

Can you see the back of my neck as you stand before me?
You close your eyes, say *I see it.*
I believe you, my reason is weakening.
I believe my eyes,
I believe my wound exists,
I believe we stand full-real and bleeding before the ten thousand.
We won't escape the gaze of the ten thousand.

ADDRESS ON THE TENTH DAY
for J. D.

This morning all non-coffee energy comes from having slept in
your blue shirt.

Soon we will fly north and see a glacier: proof that poignancy
can be planned.

Before the needle (*poignard*) goes in, we must ride in an airplane,
but airplanes also are poignant. Liftoff: the moment that flying
stops being a metaphor.

Quiet, with you. Said Flaubert: *Live your life quietly so you can be
savage in your work.*

Flaubert called his study, where he wrote, his shouting room
(*gueuloir*). While he wrote, it is said, he made a lot of noise.

I trust you to watch over me in my study, and I will watch over you.

In the eleventh century, a French priest met the devil, disguised
as a seal, who offered to carry him to Iceland. When they
were within sight of land, the priest brained the devil with a
psalter and swam safely to shore.

In Iceland we will eat seal meat as if to save the family of man.
We will pick up from the street the hands of the tower clocks
that blow down in the wind.

We will observe the near-black despair of summer.

At this particular moment in the historical cycle, it's hard to find
despair that contributes in a valuable way to a genre that's
seen a lot of derivative despair.

And yours is mysterious even to you. It's a discovery I may never make.

Yet when it's all over with no artifact save a hunk of reindeer cheese in the bottom of the suitcase,

the thermal pool will hide a mystery that will draw people to it and fill them with a horror they will find beautiful, even if the word does not occur to them.

There is a dictionary, you can put your hand in it.
It is boiling hot, in it there grows an explicit love
And a new word describing your hand. It happens very fast.
The word sounds variously depending on the light.
Light, you keep coming back differently unknowable,
And I love that. Bootleggers and pirates, here they are with their
    hands,
They wait their turns. Some want to put their cocks in the
    dictionary,
Which is wrong. The dictionary does not need their sperm.
They touch it! You are shining again today, light.
I put my hand in, I take it out, I am thinking about you.
The sound is inside the head and I see what I have become:
The sound is in the God-producing head.

WILL WE?

My favorite euphemism for death is *the future*.

Vermeer's kitchen maid is not the most famous painting in the
Rijksmuseum though she pours her milk perfectly and milk
poured no more slowly then than it does now.

In Cleveland, Aunt Jean offers me a Vantage and teaches me a
game of solitaire called *The Queen Goes into the Woods*.

The older I get, the more I can discard.

Will we never live together in the round house?

TIRED

I'm tired of looking at this blonde's well-formed ass
But she sure can weed a garden.
Does she know I dream about her white eyelashes?
Does she know all ambition has the same source?
The gray bird describes a shape,
The deer bounces up a hill,
Many animals walk on the earth and silence me.
Thanks, gravity.
Thanks, big-ass blonde.
Weed away! Let the light burn you,
The sun distract you from the blazing world!
For death is coming! And love will be new!

KITTY IN THE SNOW

Meanwhile I fuck this sculpture
In my mind until it melts, then stop.
Mmm, cold.
At the party I talk to everyone's honey
And sip poison and then go home,
Get shitfaced, and get it on with myself.
I'm so good, I give it to myself every bad way I know.
I whisper in my ear as I come:
Sarah Manguso, you're a damn fine lover.
Maybe someday we can be together, too.

Waking Up

One day I woke up and had everything I wanted right there
In the apartment so I got a tattoo of the apartment

I thought I should move
I thought I should slow down
The speed of writing I went from electronic

To manual to notebook I bought
Some clay in which to sculpt the text
Of my poems as they occurred

Suddenly appeared the face from my last dream
It sang a little song about its ideas
Which I tried to sculpt at the speed it sang them

Sing to me little face
Sing of the little faces you remember from life

Better to Shed No Light on the Mystery Than to Shed Bad Light

The zeros gather on the hill and start to bleat:

If I'm not a one, what am I?

Come here, little zero!
and together we can invent one.

I can bury my face in your soft wool.

Woolly zero, someday I will make a coat of you!

There is only facility and retribution.
The day I woke up giggling was the day I gave up controlling my
    perversion:
That was one bad dream.
Why is the heart *broken* and not squashed, flattened, or wrung out?
Would you wring out an icicle?
I give up writing about twice a day, just to keep things fresh.
I write myself a citation every time I break the rule and start
    writing again.
Sometimes I write a citation just so I can write a citation.

They Are Unlike Us in Almost Every Other Way

The light was shooting out of my eyes again.
I had a tattoo on my wrist, it was cool,
It meant I was all-powerful.
My name terrified me, I whispered it.
Every metaphor was the one about drugs.
Spaghetti alla carbonara! nothing was safe from that metaphor.
Every pretty good idea begins with the statue of a man
The moment before the snakebite.
But I am already in the next moment,
Circulating pink venom ahead of schedule.
And yet I can't leave my room. Everything is in it already.
What is it like? It isn't like anything. It already is everything.

WICKEDEST MAN

I met the wickedest man in the world,
He threw a deck of cards at me and fucked me everywhere.
I was ready for it. I didn't need props,
I couldn't wait for my head to start aching like the Black Hills.
I walked over the bald ground with the wickedest man
And we took pictures of ourselves as we imagined
Having already burned it. The wickedest man
Tied me to the track and stopped the train.
After that we attended a council of tears
Behind a house, I am walking toward it moving my hips
Like a born-again whore, there is darkness in that house.
I understand now: I am to live there into my dotage
Kneeling and whispering incantations in the corners
And waiting for the wickedest man.
I am walking toward it, it is so close now.
I see I am nothing like this house.
It is leaning toward me, I think it is happy I am finally home.
I am ready for the windows to break and nothing
To come out but a dust that kills you and a crying sound:
My inhabitant!

NATURE

I'm walking through the metal detector,
The alarm is sounding, my hand is waving.
My hand is waving as I walk through the beautiful
Nature place. We're standing in a bird blind,
No birds but deer, one big one small,
They don't see me or my hand.
The deer eat the seeds that have fallen
In storms or storms of birds.
I'm finished talking about the old things, no more
Gray birds, hands, no more expectation.
The small crumbly spirals are the earthworms' digestion.
All the earth was like this once
Or more than once. I don't take your hand in the bird blind,
I don't take anything I'm afraid of ruining it.
I go back to the room where my friend always coughs
And smokes, having seen no birds. I call her *Bird*.
I'm proud of my limited number of experiences.
I'm ready to go on to the next ones, or the ones
That remind me of the birds in these.

I am the postmaster. I have 900 boxes. And I drive under the bridges in my truck and the hearts are alive, beating in their boxes, and I'm driving over the bridges in love with destiny and in charge of the 900 hearts.

To faint with desire is the only good thing. We crave to measure the strength of it, but there is no mercury thermometer, no tall graduate filled with floating predictors.

In my experience, the dream of love wears off in a week, but in that week your mind is a new mind.

I see the people in their purple suits, sitting down and standing up. Some of them are holding their hearts.

So much for immortality. After he died, Keats's friends couldn't agree on what color his eyes had been.

Now, if only the boxes would open up and beat their one-word answer.

Now, if the hearts would open up and show us their pink insides...

LOVE LETTER (CLOUDS)
for B. H.

I didn't fall in love. I fell through it:

Came out the other side moments later, hands full of matter, waking up from the dream of a bullet tearing through the middle of my body.

I no longer understand anything for longer than a long moment, or the time it takes to receive the shot.

This kind of gravity is like falling through a cloud, forgetting it all, and then being told about it later. *On the day you fell through a cloud...*

It must be true. If it were not, then when did these strands of silver netting attach to my hair?

The problem was finding that you were real and not just a dream of clouds.

If you weren't real, I would address this letter to one of two entities: myself, or everyone else. The effect would be equivalent.

The act of falling happens in time. That is, it takes long enough for the falling to shear away from the moments before and the moments after, long enough for one to have thought *I am falling. I have been falling. I continue to fall.*

Falling through a ring, in this case, would not mean falling through the center of the annulus—a planet floats there. Falling through the ring means falling through the spaces between the objects that together make the ring.

On the way through, clasp your fists around the universe:

Nothing but ice-gravel.

But open your hands when you reach the other side. Quickly, before it melts.

What did I leave you?

BURNING

I want to stick my hand in the energy!
The brightness that outstays its welcome,

That rides the lightning and has to do with God.
I want to stick my hand in a Bunsen burner

And watch the flame bore through it
Like a Jesus nail. I want to light my lamp at the tip

Of the inside violet blue and attach it to the underside
Of you and when you crawled the nine hundred miles

To Massapequa I would be shouting on the side
Of the riverbank, and you wonder why I'm waving

My arms and opening my mouth wide
And throwing red fire into the low branches.

HAND MODEL

Up to my eyes in ups
I practice various hand poses
As a way of appreciating my hands.

It's a sweet hard life, hair blowing everywhere.
I am a man.
My hands are famous and I hate my life.
But today the studio floor is covered in ladies
Who will be dead of aortic aneurysms within the year
And will waft beautifully into Hell
Which is the only way out of this place,
My best hearts, my sisters,
Take me below.

An Idea with No Bodily Counterpart

He got to the world where images were real,
Where death came and scared him back to life.
It drank his blood.
He suffered some more, he liked it.
He quieted down to the point where he could finally hear,
And he heard 1,000 windows scraping open or shut.
He heard his best ideas gathering outside him as trees,
And he heard apes walking among them.
He could hear them getting lost in the big forest.
Now they are absolutely gone.

Invocation to the Muse

Delacroix, whose name is literal but false, made a painting called *Milton Dictating* Paradise Lost *to His Daughters.*

Milton was blind when he did his dictating, and in the picture, he's turned away from the ardent daughters.

His eyes are closed. He looks French.

The blonde looks panicky. She has no idea what she's about to write down.

The point is, neither does Milton, but he looks calm.

Flaubert writes: *To seek to imitate the methods of geniuses would be fatal. They are great for the very reason that they have no methods.*

When you made me a tape and called it *Rock and Roll Will Never Die,* you weren't talking about rock and roll.

The tape is made from old LPs and is full of static. Like Delacroix's name, this is dishonest but beautiful.

You are dishonest, too. And your beautiful blond hair.

Muse, see what I think about. I need you. Rock and roll describes me literally: *I wish you were here.*

Muse, come out into this power ballad. I would give you a backstage pass, Muse. I would offer you my best amp, and I would praise you.

I would make empty promises. I would say things to you in French.

And when I tired of you, you would point to the sky, to the sun, and remind me that Milton's memory couldn't have been that good without a little help.

HELL

The second-hardest thing I have to do is not be longing's slave.

Hell is that. Hell is that, others, having a job, and not having a
   job. Hell is thinking continually of those who were truly
   great.

Hell is the moment you realize you were ignorant of the fact,
   when it was true, that you were not yet ruined by desire.

The kind of music I want to continue hearing after I'm dead is the
   kind that makes me think I'll be capable of hearing it then.

There is music in Hell. Wind of desolation! It blows past the egg-
   eyed statues. The canopic jars are full of secrets.

The wind blows through me. I open my mouth to speak.

I recite the list of people I have copulated with. It does not take
   long. I say the names of my imaginary children. I call out
   four-syllable words beginning with B. This is how I stay
   alive.

Beelzebub. Brachiosaur. Bubble-headed. I don't know how I stay
   alive. What I do know is that there is a light, far above us,
   that goes out when we die,

and that in Hell there is a gray tulip that grows without any sun.
   It reminds me of everything I failed at,

and I water it carefully. It is all I have to remind me of you.

ASTRONOMICAL PROJECTION

If people were sent to live on the moon, they would yell with grief for their wet little planet. But silently—no noise allowed on the moon.

What happens on Earth? Confusion of all sorts. A big party in Piedmont where people fall into the canals with their dogs. Somehow they get from the canals to the libraries,

where the books are full of our history. The cheerleaders' teeth are shiny. They live in a town, and it is a decent town. You live there.

The people in the book are from another time. But their time, their planet, did not, in time, become yours.

Since your own story does not warrant nostalgia, you are in mourning for theirs.

THE ONLY THING TO PRAY FOR IS FIRE

The new age came. I invited it inside.

By the end of the week it had settled in the cellar.

One day it knocked on the sewing-room door and made as if to
  speak.

I waited, my mouth full of pins.

You seem to be making a quilt, it said.

I was only lengthening a pair of pants, but I said nothing.

*You have been waiting for me to speak. Now that I am speaking you
  believe a new age is here.*

I put the pants into the basket.

*When the quilt is finished I will get under it with you—together we
  will bring about a new age! But first you will need to summon
  the quilt-making fire...*

The boy speaks in Russian (I understand him neither in the dream nor in real life). He opens his eyes and looks at me, apologizing in English for keeping them closed.

When I wake up I think he must have seen me. But when I kiss him he looks surprised, as if he were blind.

The night I met you I wrote: *It is possible I have imagined my entire life.*

•

My great-grandmother's lamp is mine now. It is made of rose quartz—that is, it is made of poetry.

More poetry: A coin you dropped when you took your pants off is still on the floor. Please come back and pick it up.

More: The scar on my hand I got cleaning the house for you has outlasted you. In this way you are indelible, but only as long as I have my hand.

Here.
Is what it is because of where the speaker is standing.

Hades.
Literally, "the unseen."

The World.
A metaphor lurching toward its thing.

Baffling Wind.
A light wind that frequently shifts from one point to another.

Fame.
Though not a jellyfish itself, looks as if it's made of jellyfish.

Democracy.
If enough people vote, any lake can become great.

Plastic Bags.
Hang in the branches, flapping like the end of the reel. The
    movie is about you.

There.
All I ever wanted to do was look at you.

THINGS I HAVE LEARNED

History.
My teacher can barely tell the story of Samuel Taylor Coleridge's
    six dead brothers and his (Coleridge's) getting thrown out
    of the army for insanity—that is, for not being able to ride a
    horse or shoot straight.

Artists.
Asked in the early 1940s why he didn't work from nature, Jackson
    Pollock replied: *I am nature.*

Working.
After a friend has been out of school for a year, he says to me:
    Eventually I stopped keeping track of how stupid I was getting.

Leaves.
The sight of leaves blowing in the street makes you think you
    hear leaves blowing in the street, but only if you have heard
    them before.

Love.
I think I know what it is that makes me love him, but someday
    he will die. This makes me love him less, but only for a
    moment.

Plagiarism.
Planet TMR-1C thus seems destined to be a *rogue planet,* detached
    from any star and drifting forever outward. It may be that this
    planet's lonely fate is shared by many similar bodies drifting
    aimlessly through space, astronomers speculated Thursday.
    God help me, but I copied this from the newspaper.

Mortality.
William Blake taught his wife, Catherine, how to read and how
to operate a printing press. He dreamed of a man who taught
him how to paint. When he awoke, he painted pictures of
him.

A Final Love Poem

After ending it, I'm less sad about my loneliness than about his, which I can never know the dimensions of.

Someone I meet in a bar tells me that one of my poems, a poem about the apocalypse, is a good love poem. It cures me of the need to write love poems.

The soap opera teen says: *There is no such thing as love. There is only misunderstanding and cruelty.*

The soap opera mother says: *Just don't wait too long.*

Most people would rather convince themselves of being in love than of being happy, just as most people would rather believe they are talking to others when talking to themselves.

I have never been what people call an *outdoorsman*—I have been hiking in the mountains exactly twice—but what bothers me is the near certainty that I will not die out of doors.

After hearing her deliberations for weeks, I advise my friend to sleep with the German, since all the universe will be the same before as it is after she sleeps with him—except, of course, for the fact that she will have slept with the German.

Whatever the lover gives to you just before parting, when you first meet, when you end it, will be significant, since anything may be used as a metaphor for anything else.

Where beauty is, there you see yourself.

As I age, I find fewer things beautiful. The number of possibilities for my ultimate self decreases as time passes. It is possible that, the moment before my death, I will find exactly one thing beautiful.

When I am dead I won't remember what it was that ruined me, or how death once seemed no worse than ruin.

TELL ME, TELL ME WHO...

One day I was incapable of inventing new words.
I put my head in a sling and tried to go on, business as usual.

The book of love? Two volumes lying on the bed,
Maybe mystery novels, touching.

Where you are, I once was. All we did was written down.
This made it beautiful and different.

Now it is no longer real.
Soon it will never have happened.

Painting Dream

The dream is about the various motions.
The dream is that the eyes move by themselves.
Nothing seizes them
And they move like selves.
Things seen are never finished
And in the dream they are finished.

Waving a brush, for example, covers any surface.
Something lies underneath—
If only there were the proper scraping tool.
The thought alone reveals the dreamer's body underneath.
The dreamer imagines himself dead.
In the dream, there is such a thing as being dead.

In the dream, excellent paintings lie in stacks.

The Idea of Italy

I call the idea *Italy* so as not to frighten it.
It sweats gently from its forehead.

It wants to trust me with its life.
Come, Sardinia!

Let me bathe in your little sea.
Let me stand with one foot on you and one on Sicily.

I am flying east.
The closer Italy comes, the more joy I feel.

The most mysterious part of Italy is Pompeii.
The sign for its ruins: three dots, one on top of two.

The country's face: written over with the names the ancients gave it.
What they said, we believe. We don't know what else to believe.

The idea of Italy is a sort of ancient blue.
It makes me smile, sometimes, with its *commedia dell'arte*.

Once I tried to break off part of it
but that only made it more beautiful.

I went to France and it was still there—
The very idea of Italy!

Alas, They Sighed, You Were Not Like Us

For once they had nothing to say about my death
And I killed them.
After that I put on a Neil Young record in my poem because he
  used to write in fevers
And because there's something about beauty that's always going
  to be a problem.

They told me if I played "Cinnamon Girl" enough times, they
  would love me.
They didn't have to hold me
And they sent me money and macrame belts
Spelling the words *Jesus* and *O to Know Your Dark Uplifted Heart.*
I loved them
And I was listening to myself
And writing down what I heard.
They were pretty sure it was about them.

I Don't Know to Call It Bitterness or Joy

Beautiful loss, stand and wait just a little longer. Soon I'll have spent my life trying to find you.

Amusement speeds me to my death. Others bury themselves alive in money.

My prayer's the one on its knees begging for its life.

My prayer's the one holding the sparkler, writing itself in the air.

I can make out the remains of its shining tail. *And last, save the animals from the future of the kingdom...*

Which stories of farms are the ones that can save me?

Which farms can save me?

In their wooden stalls, the critters are standing and chewing.

I am writing about them. I am looking at them sidewise, from the doorway, sobbing.

The animal I rescue is the animal I tear out of my own belly.

New year, see how I need you. Beautiful destroyer, let us remember only the future.

Kneeling behind the barn, I take a breath and pray.

I hear myself in my need. I receive my prayer with kindness and equanimity.

Tomorrow I bury the meat and the bones.

That we rode harder into the wind,
That the story got told,
That the broken candies were eaten first,
That they were eaten last,
That all subjects grew extinct eventually,
That in the inn I ruined our lives,
That in the barn I tried to save them,
That I failed,
That per Fitzgerald *the manner remains intact for some time after
    the morale cracks,*
That in the *interregna* all suffer equally,
That the languages we are born ready to speak leave us one by one,
That unless we're actively procreating we're acting metaphorically,
That I've never been to France,
That I've been to Ohio,
That I remember almost nothing I did there,
That it is meaningless to say *I liked that,*
That emotions accumulate into a few categories,
That each new one is itself plus everything *like itself,*
That when animals act like people we love them more,
That when they do we want them never to stop,
That we give them the names we wish we had,
That men have children and manufacture new mothers,
That I anticipate escaping my fate or not,
That I anticipate the future by never buying groceries,
That I know the flesh is incidental but keep so many photographs,
That the story gets told,
That it was the reason for these various movements.

The Trick Is Not Minding

Sometimes I'm standing in a white fire.

Sometimes I'm baking a bitter cake and whistling madly.

There's a point to going away. There's a point to bitterness.

There's a point to choosing a form and filling it completely.

Sometimes I'm sewing a shirt with the sleeves stitched shut.

How women endure being women is beyond my comprehension.

By the time the animal first leaves the nest after the big event, she
has picked the cub she will feed.

The other is already a mound of pink jelly.

When I gave birth to my death, my death thanked me.

FRIEND

My friend says *At every moment I feel as though I'm waking up from the dream which was the previous moment.*

I think I see us drifting in the dark: two bright blue, weeping icebergs.

Often I need to get onto a sled to prevent myself from tearing my chest open and betraying just what the trouble is.

The dream is just that: the thing you might have done but didn't.

The ice in the dream is cold—like real ice. But it burns, too.

Sometimes I worry that my intact, unbroken body will have smothered the fire that should have been born with it, holding onto its heel.

We decide the future before it happens. And so there is no future.

The snowman drifts on his berg, his head empty.

You imagine him forlorn. And why shouldn't you? After all, he is made in your image.

He is your friend.

When hunting, an Inuit man makes an igloo a day. Some of them have ice windows.

Once a day .he walks away from the snow house by the snow hill.

An Inuit elder who saw an airplane says *It was talked about for a long time. It was constantly talked about as something that looked like a loon that did not flap its wings.*

When the plane becomes the loon whose wings do not close, it takes something from the man he will not recover.

Invisible, it circles the snow land, burning far from the man who saw it.

Find me an igloo, melted on the inside from strangers' breath.

It was made for a day but I will save it, rescue the cold room I want incubating the last of me.

NEPENTHE

Van Gogh said he agreed with Courbet, that he couldn't paint angels because he'd never seen one—and then painted them as he saw them in paintings by the Italians.

Another of my friends is dead. His parents are doctors. There's no way to ensure your children will outlive you.

The Greeks believed in a potion to make them forget grief and suffering.

A friend writes: *My grandparents are 88 now and that makes them very quiet.*

I didn't believe in my death until last night. There was no reason to believe in it until then.

There is still no reason to believe in it.

I like it when we believe in something like *to the stars by hard ways.*

But where is the Aldebaran that I can get to only with grief?

The doctors invite me to an interminable meeting with joy,

but I'm on my knees in the music room, driving the brush tip into my open eye.

I am painting myself a bridge. I can almost see it.

A Glittering

One mourner says *if I can just get through this year* as if salvation comes in January.

Slow dance of suicides into the earth:

I see no proof there is anything else. I keep my obituary current but believe that good times are right around the corner.

A great sculpture can roll down a hill without breaking, Michelangelo is believed to have said. To determine the essential parts of a sculpture, roll it down a hill. The inessential parts will break off.

The hill, that graveyard of the inessential, is discovered by the hopeless and mistaken for the world just before they mistake themselves for David's white arms.

They are wrong. But to assume oneself essential is also wrong: a conundrum.

To be neither essential nor inessential—not to exist except as an object of someone's belief, like the good times lying right around the corner—is the only possibility.

Nothing, nobody matters.

And yet the world is full of love...

Oblivion Speaks

I am not here to ruin you.
I am already in you.
I am the work you don't do.
I am what you understand best and wordless.
I am with you in your chair and in your song.
I am what you avoid and what you stop avoiding.
I am what's left when there is nothing left.
Love me hard, pilgrim.

NOTES

"Asking for More": The second line is John Berryman's, from his 1972 *Paris Review* interview.

"This Might Be Real": The last line is adapted from Jorie Graham's poem "Underneath (13)."

"Reverence": The third line is adapted from a Zen koan.

"Justice for the Undelivered": *Islam* translates to *surrender.*

"Est, Est, Est": In one version of the legend, the 12th-century German prelate Johannes Fugger, on the way to Rome, sent his servant ahead and instructed him to mark the inns with the best wines with the word *est* (i.e., *this*). After tasting the muscato wine of Montefiascone, the page, becoming enthusiastic, wrote the word on the inn's door three times. Fugger arrived at the inn, stayed up all night drinking the lauded wine, and died in the morning.

"Waking Up" owes a debt to Donald Justice's poem "Invitation to a Ghost."

"Hand Model" owes a debt to Daniel Tiffany's poem "Come and See."

"Hell" owes a debt to Stephen Spender's poem "I think continually of those who were truly great."

"Things I Have Learned": The plagiarized portion comes from a 1998 *New York Times* article.

"The Idea of Italy": The title is adapted from the title of a 1990s-era course taught by Professor Robert Kiely at Harvard.

"Alas, They Sighed, You Were Not Like Us": The title comes from Frank O'Hara's poem "The Clown."

"The Movement of a Caravan over the Landscape": The title is adapted from the etymology of the word *narrative*.

"The Trick Is Not Minding": The title is adapted from a line believed to have been spoken by T. E. Lawrence as he held his hand over an open flame.

Born and raised in Massachusetts, Sarah Manguso lives in Brooklyn and teaches at the Pratt Institute. Her first book, *The Captain Lands in Paradise* (2002), was a *Village Voice* Favorite Book of the Year. Her poems and prose have appeared in *The American Poetry Review, The Believer, Boston Review, The London Review of Books, McSweeney's, The New Republic, The Paris Review,* and three editions of the *Best American Poetry* series. *Siste Viator* is her second book.